MY CARS, TRUCKS, PLANES AND MOTORCYCLES COLORING BOOK

THIS COLORING BOOK BELONGS TO:

_____

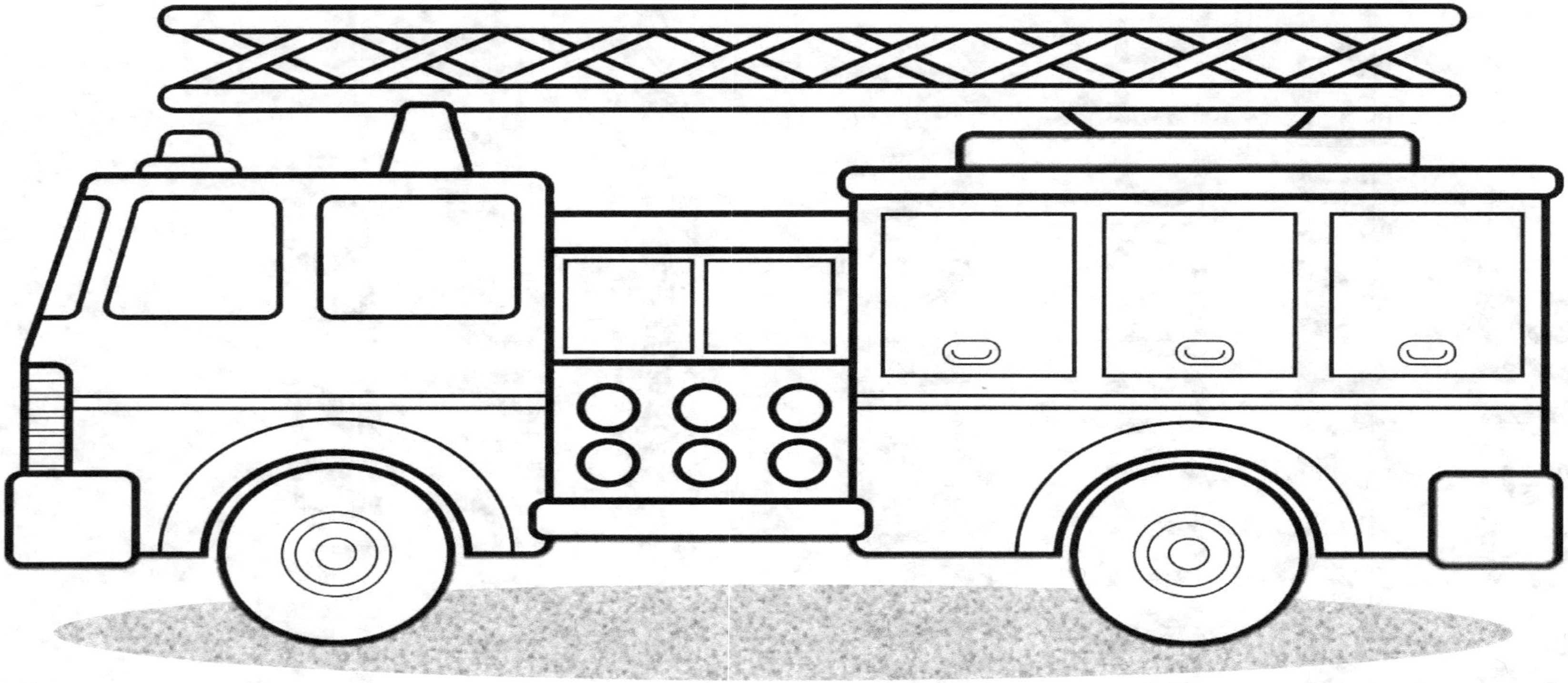

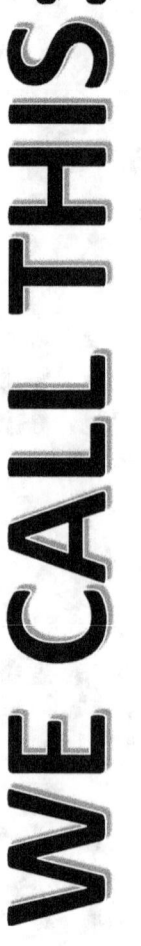

WE CALL THIS: [_____]

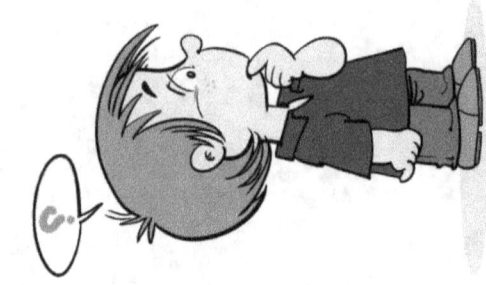

WE CALL THIS:

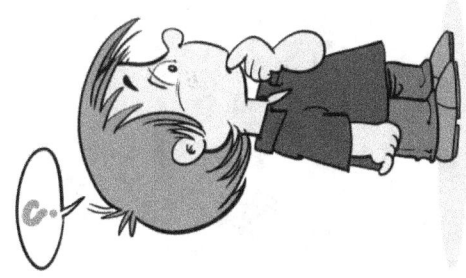

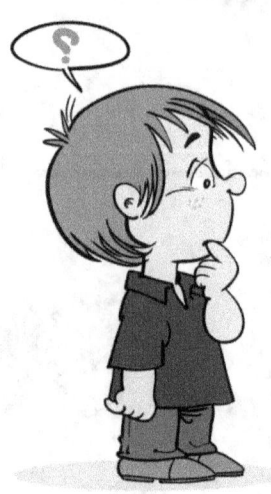

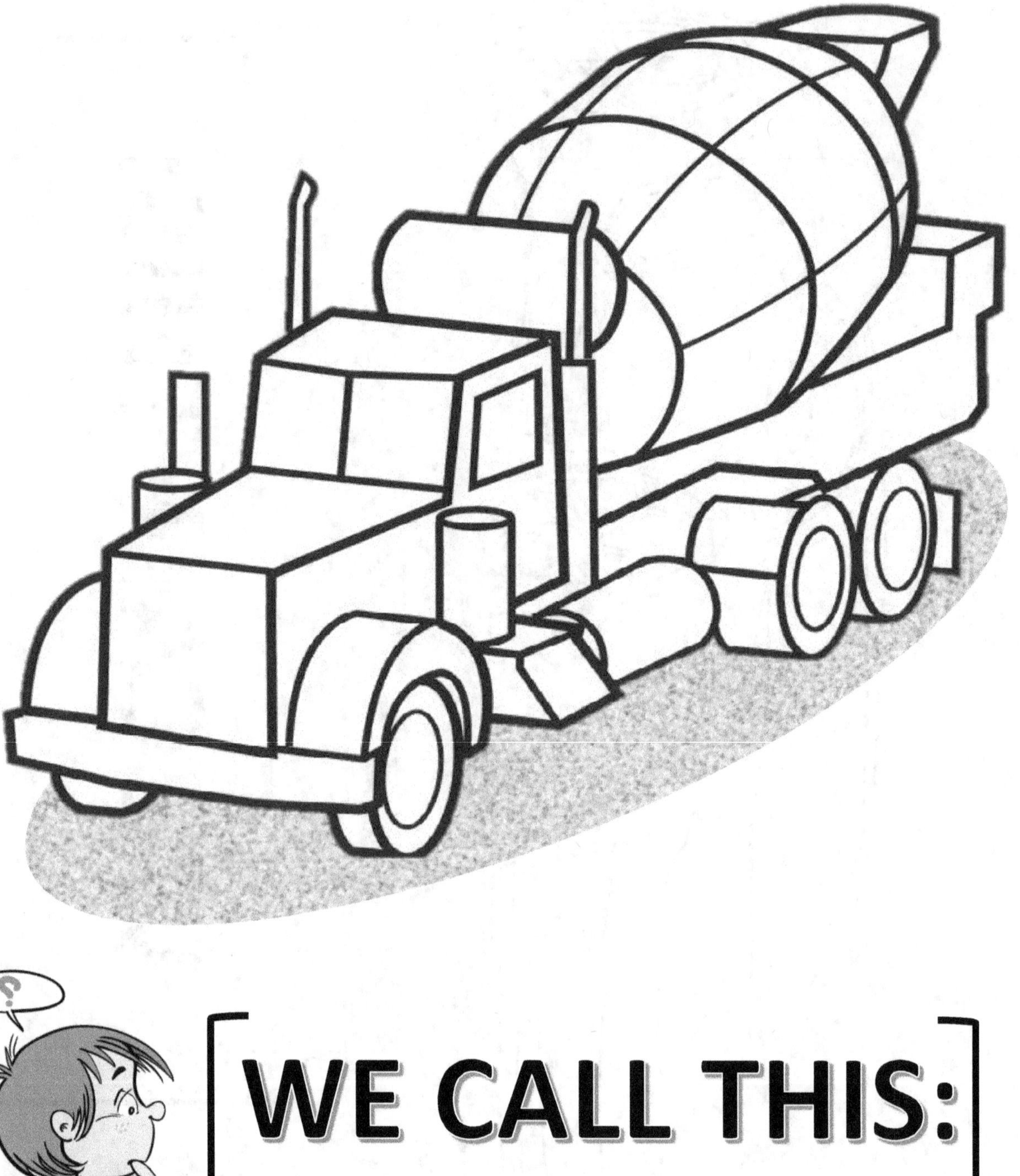

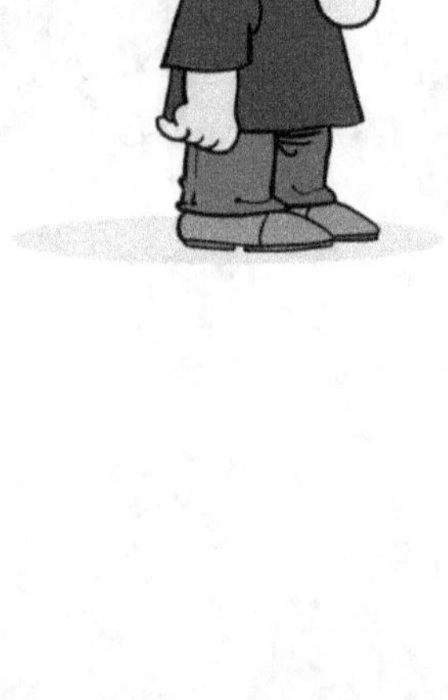

WE CALL THIS: ....

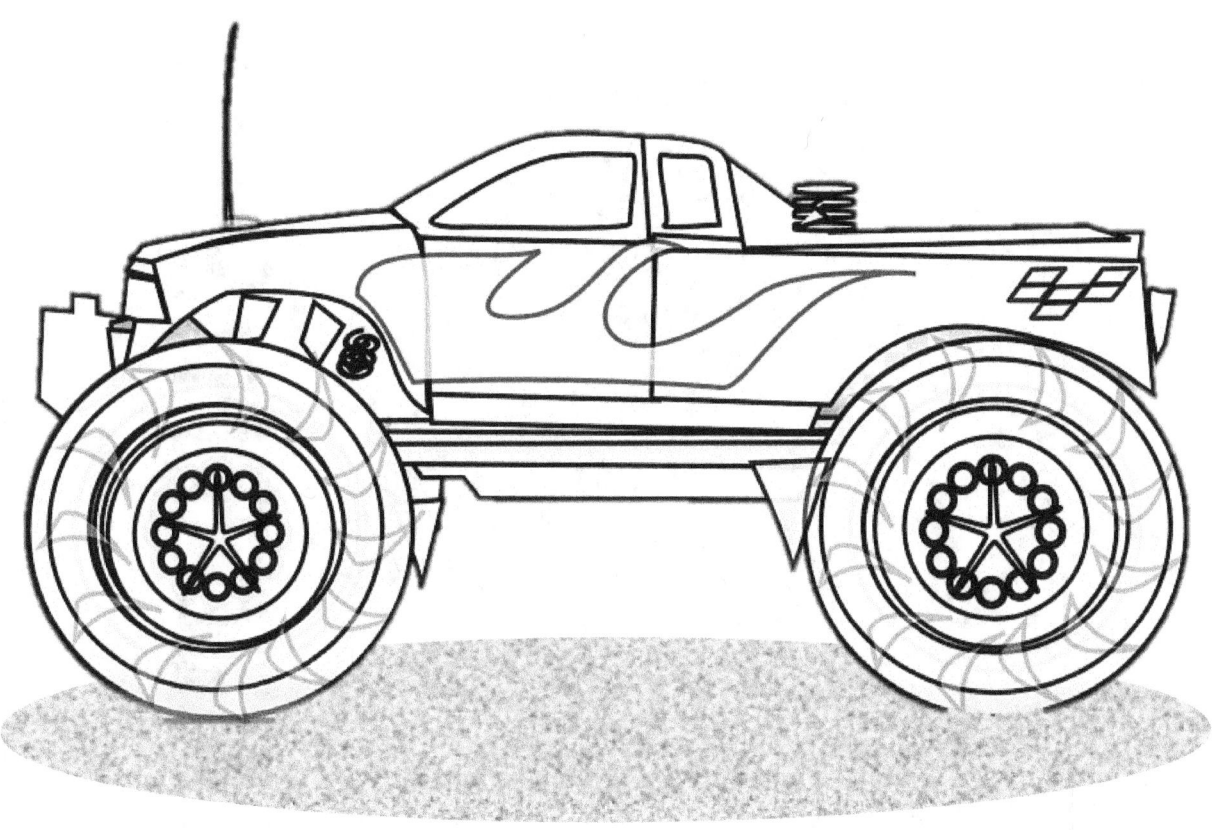

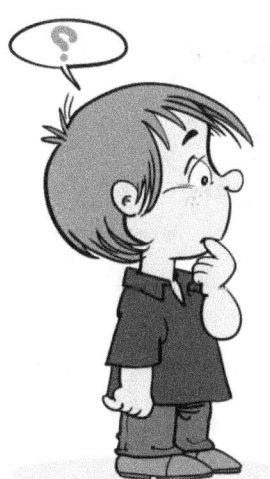 **WE CALL THIS:** _____

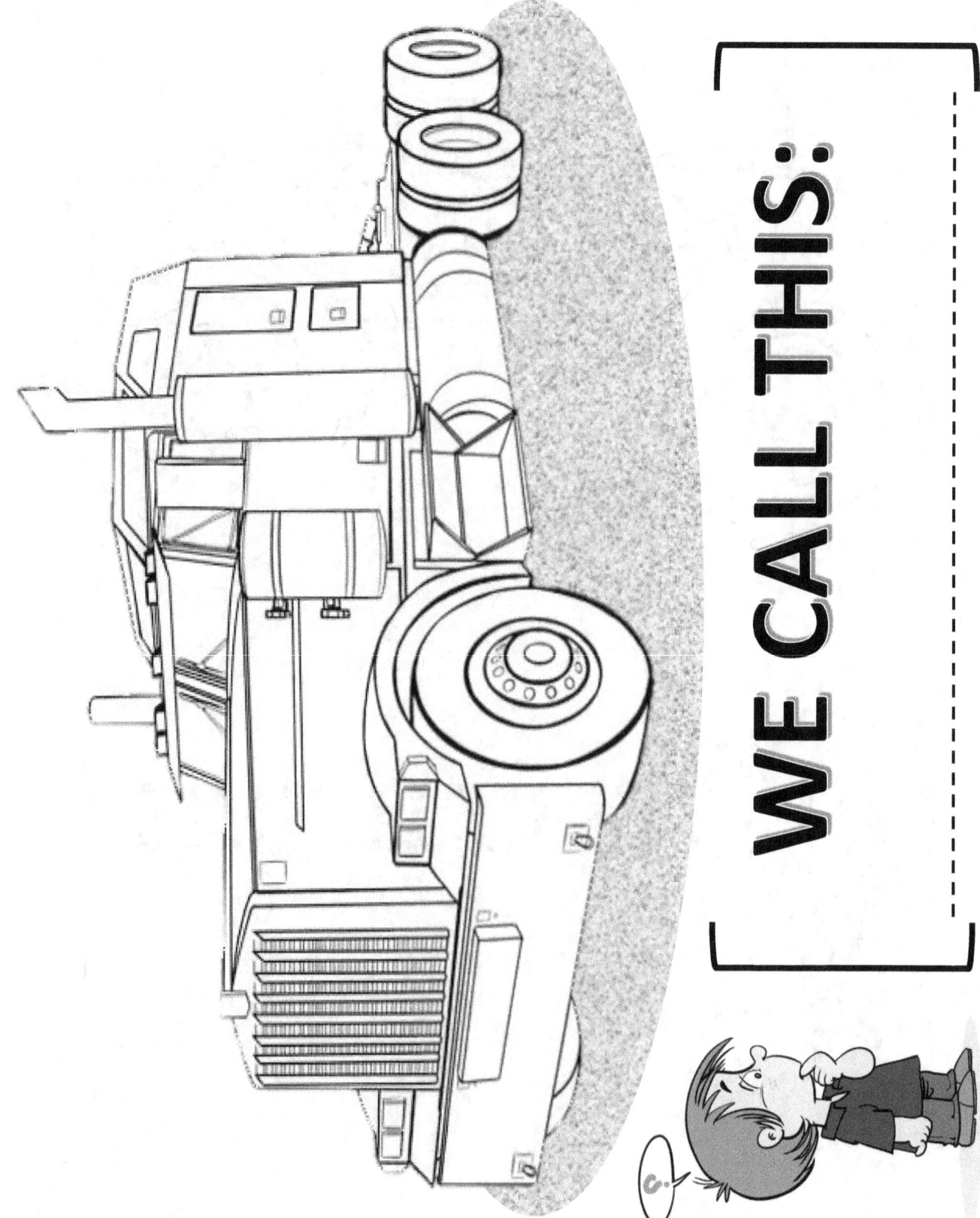

WE CALL THIS:

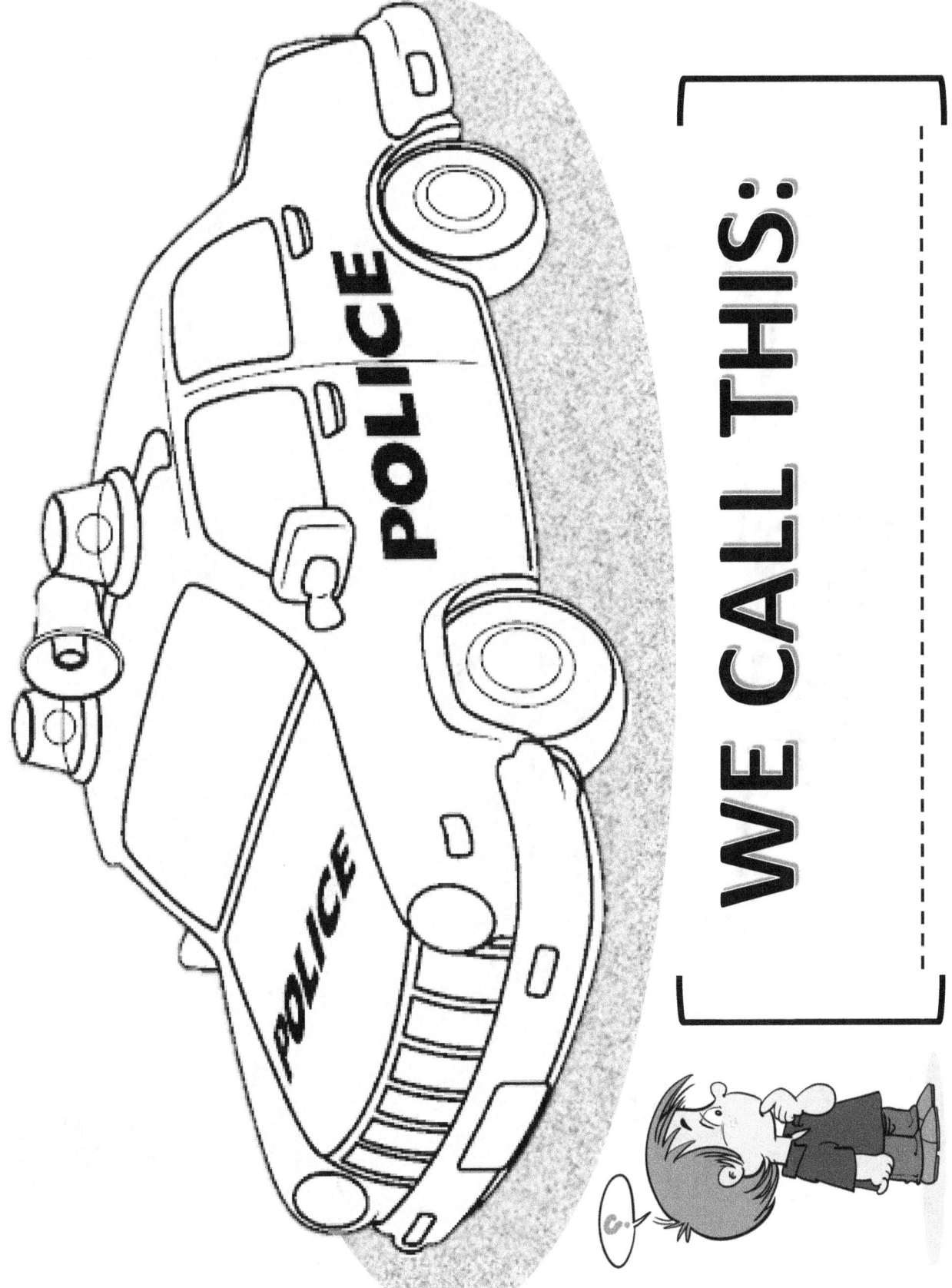

WE CALL THIS:

WE CALL THIS:

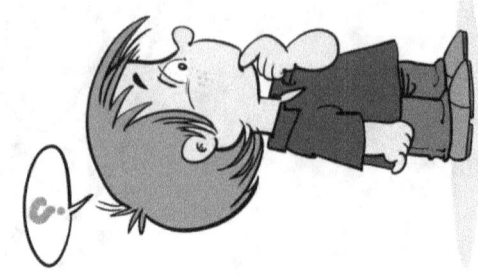

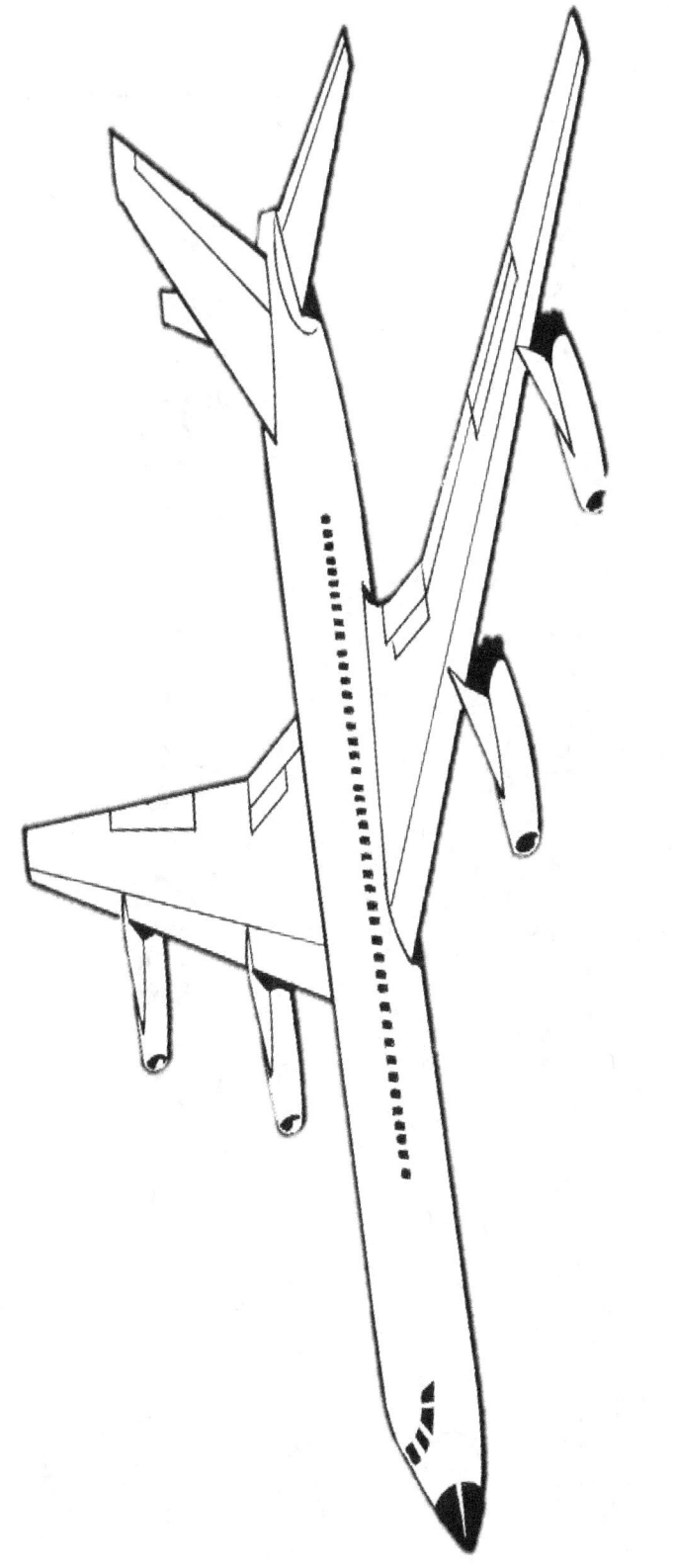

WE CALL THIS:

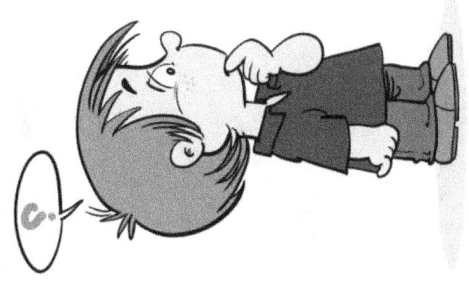

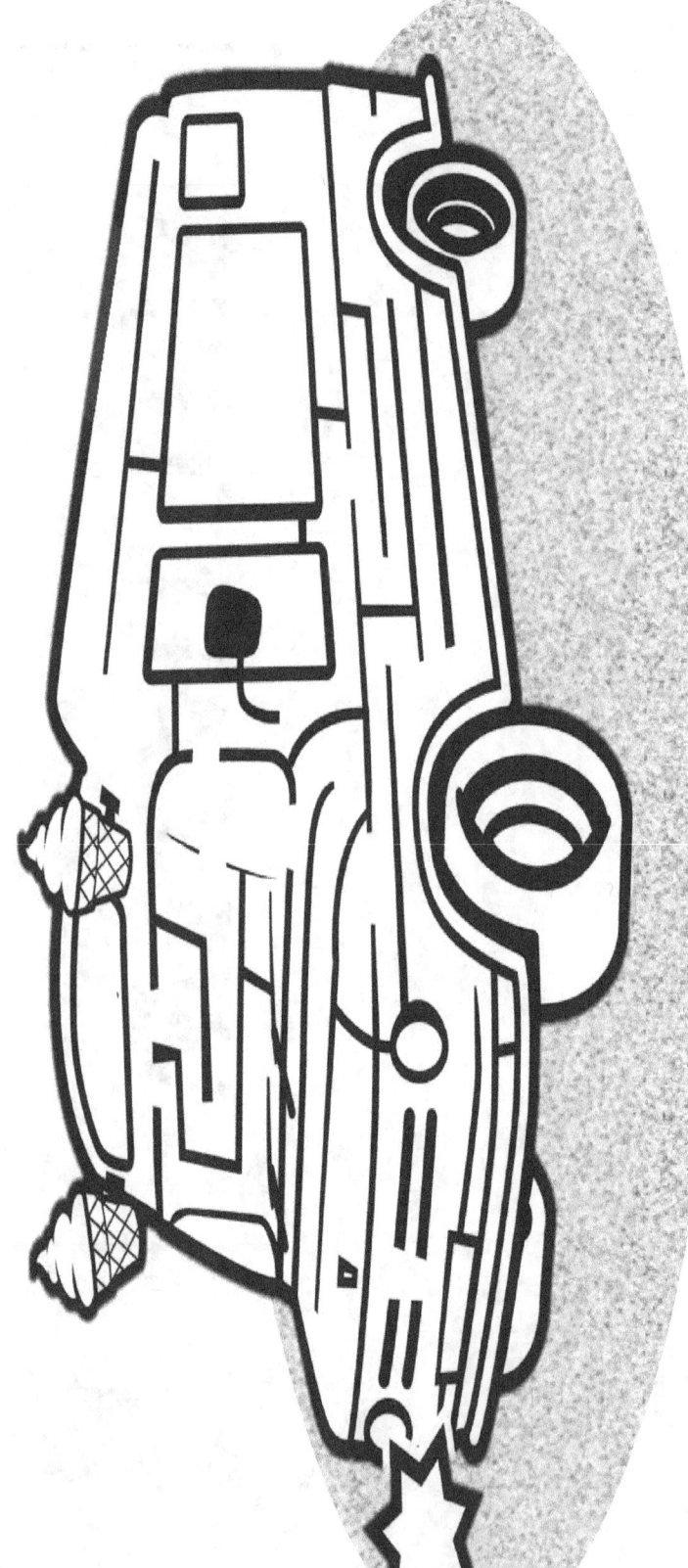

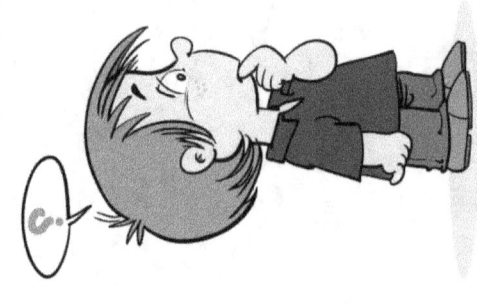

WE CALL THIS:

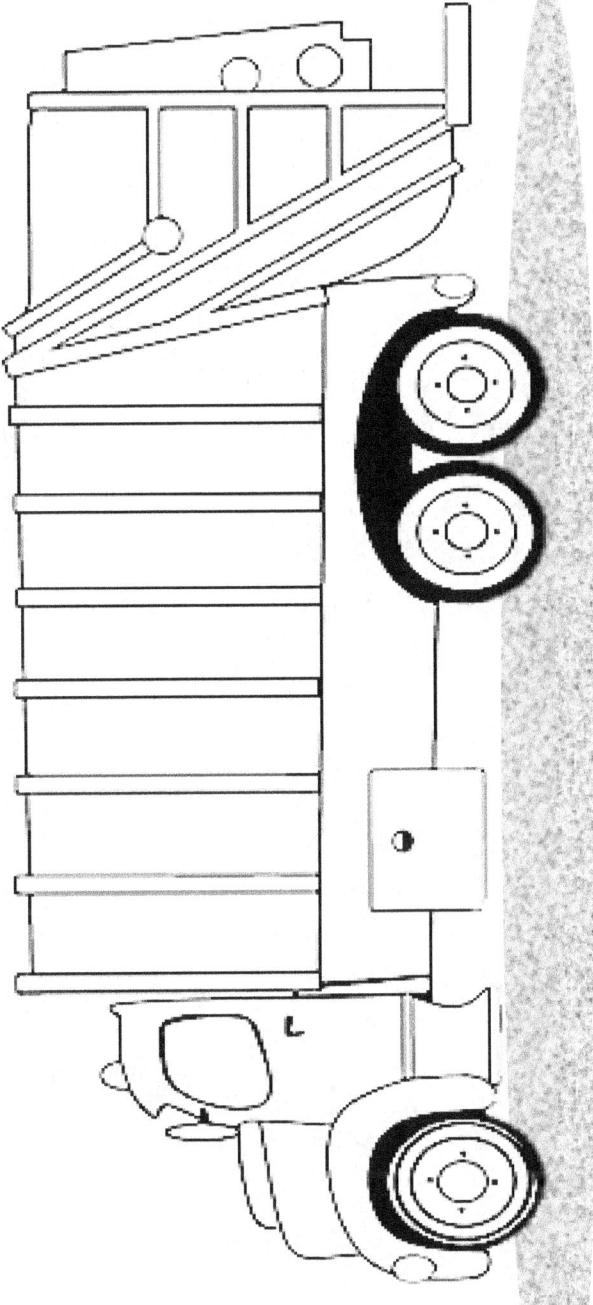

WE CALL THIS:

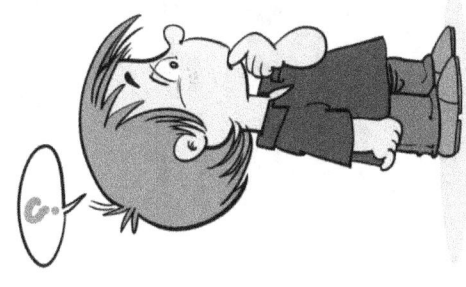

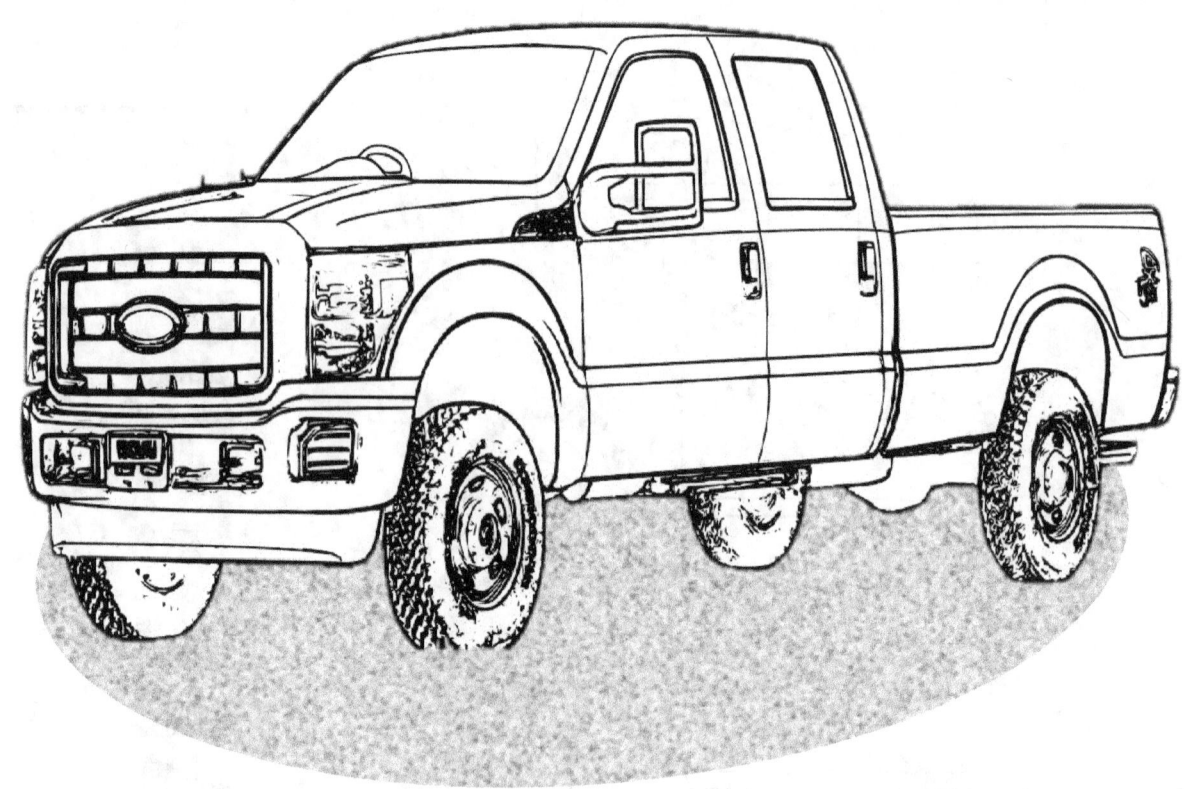

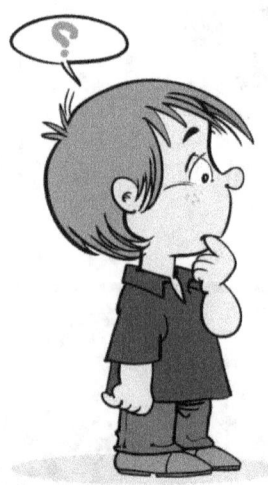

[**WE CALL THIS:**
......................................]

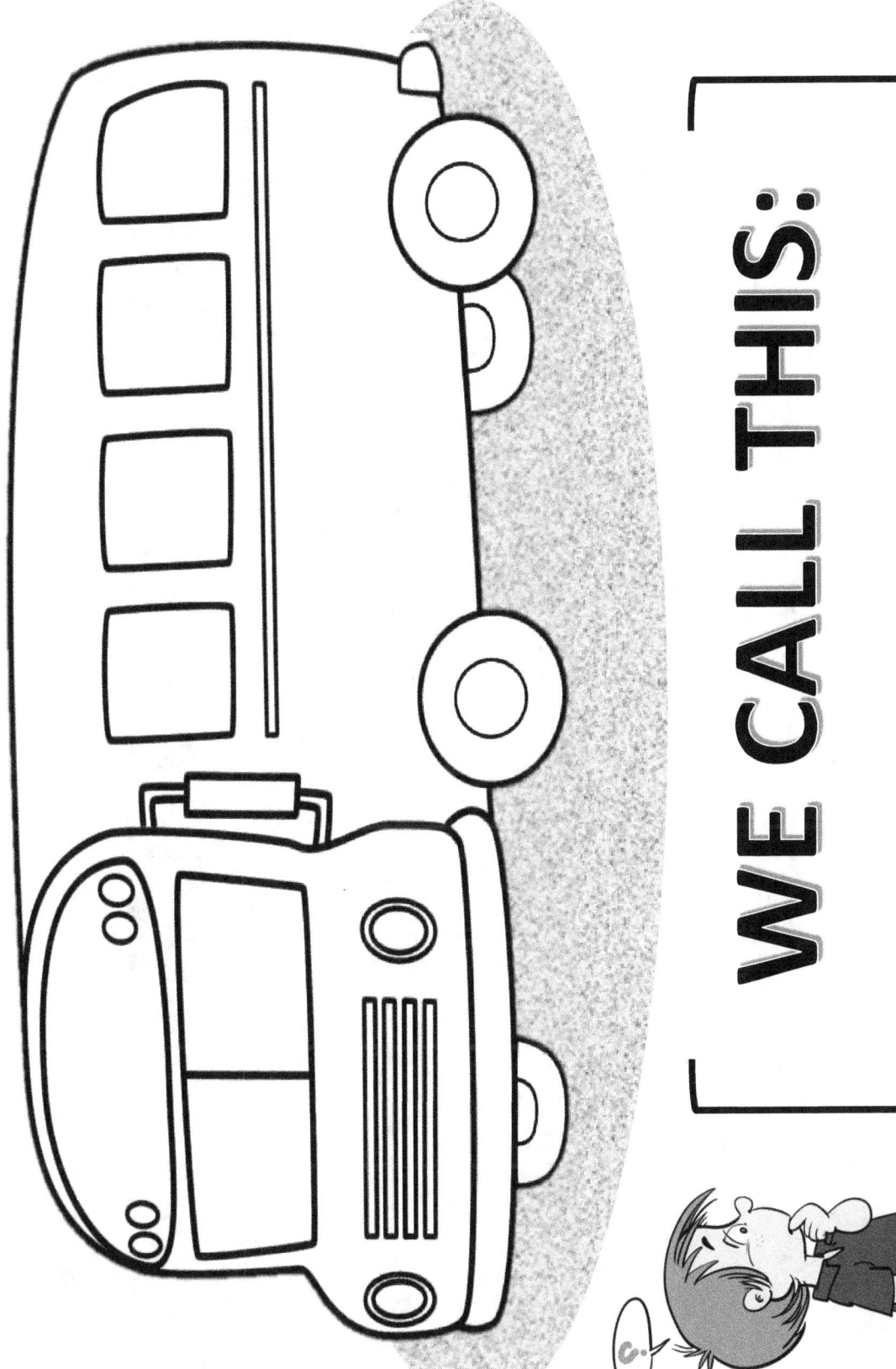

WE CALL THIS:

WE CALL THIS:

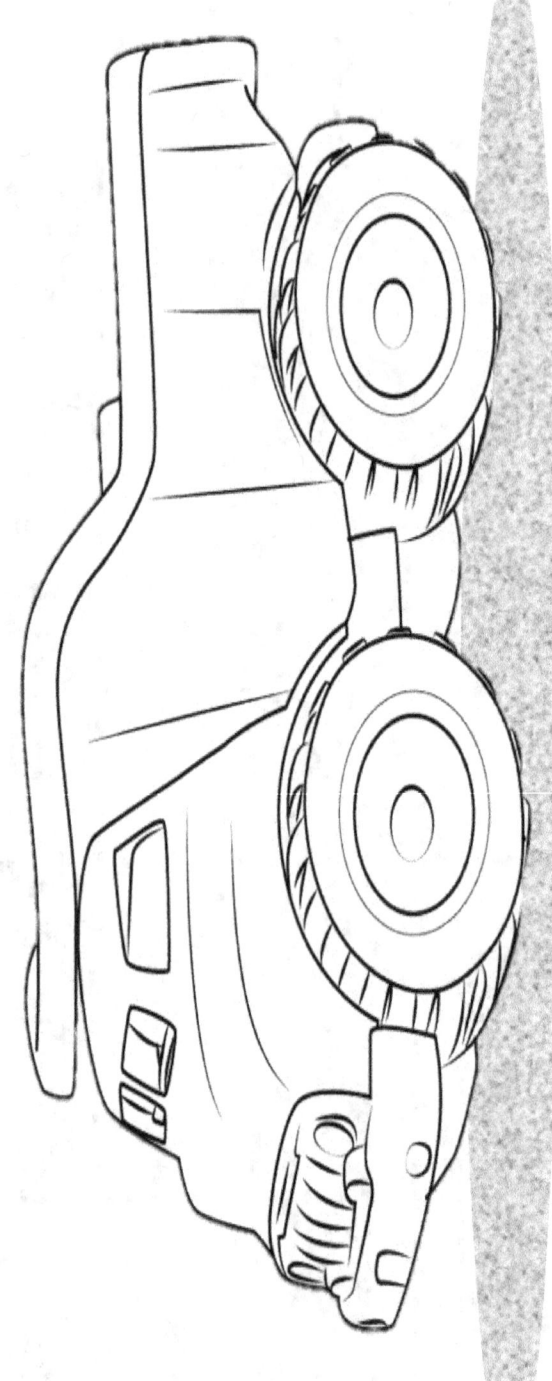
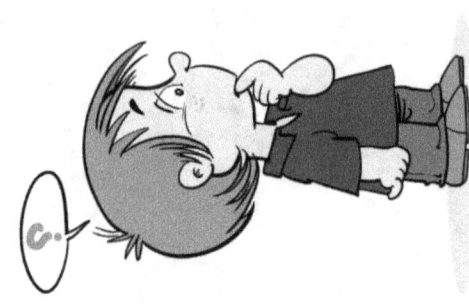

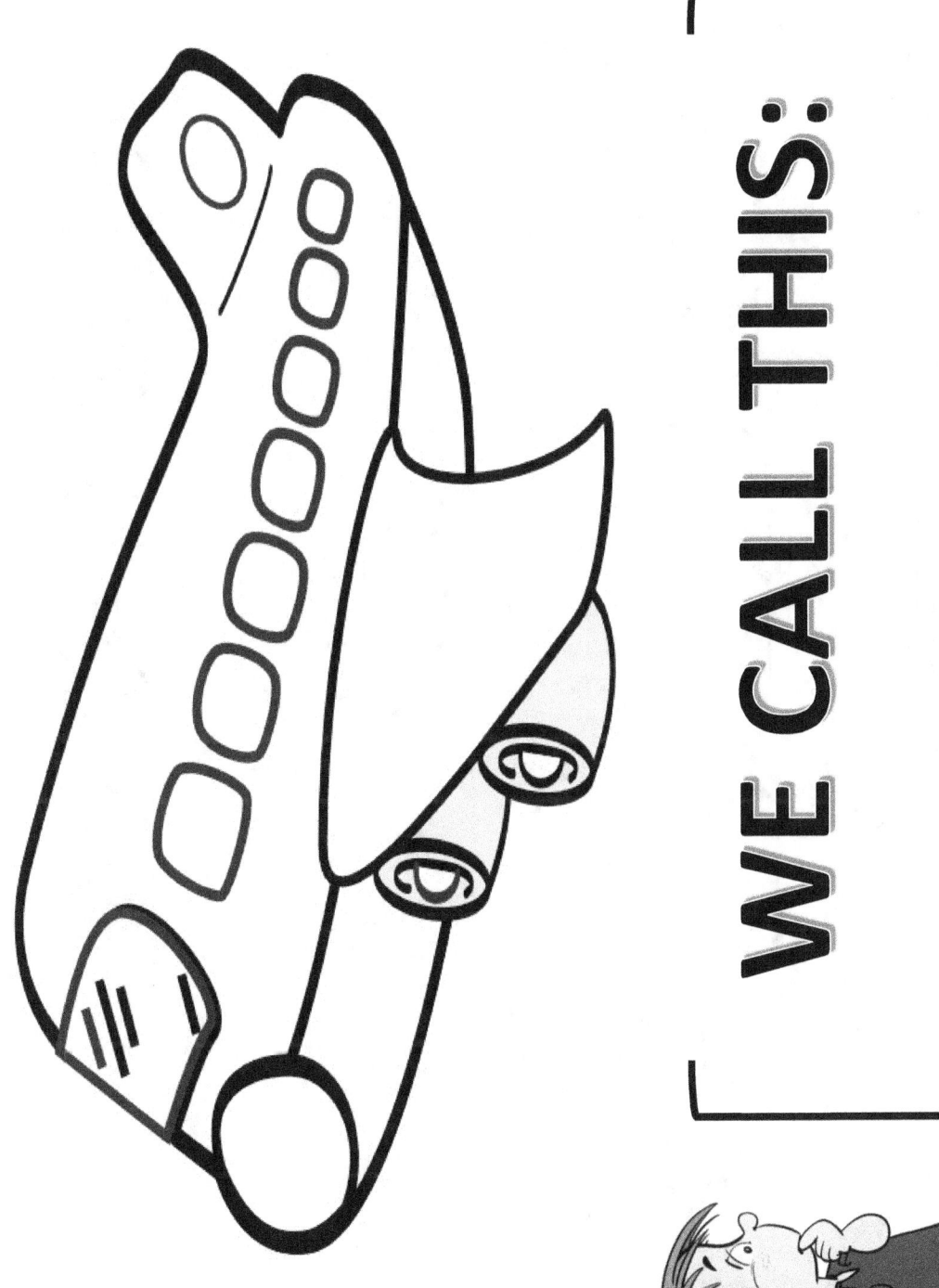

WE CALL THIS:

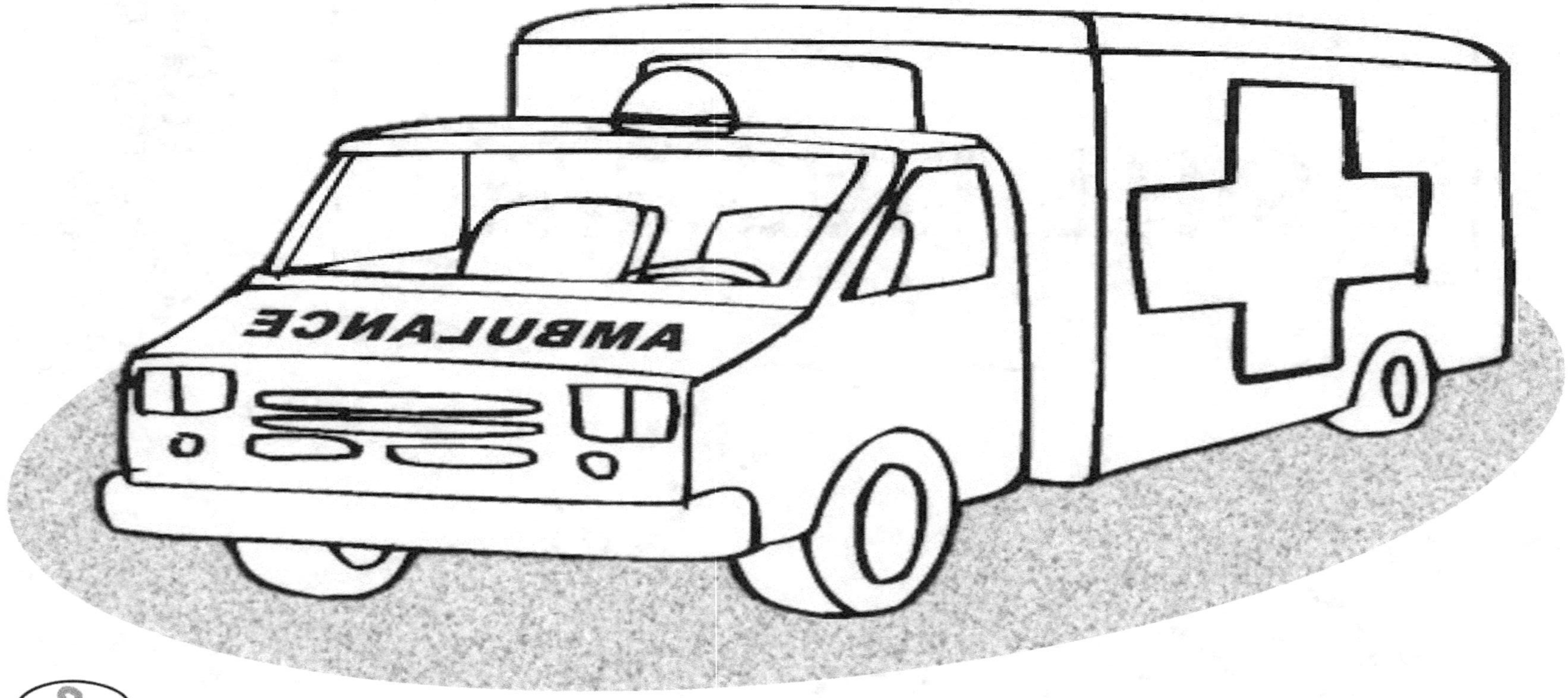

WE CALL THIS:

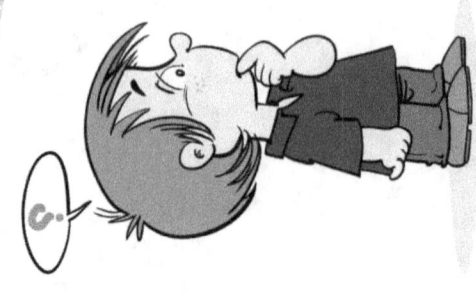

WE CALL THIS:

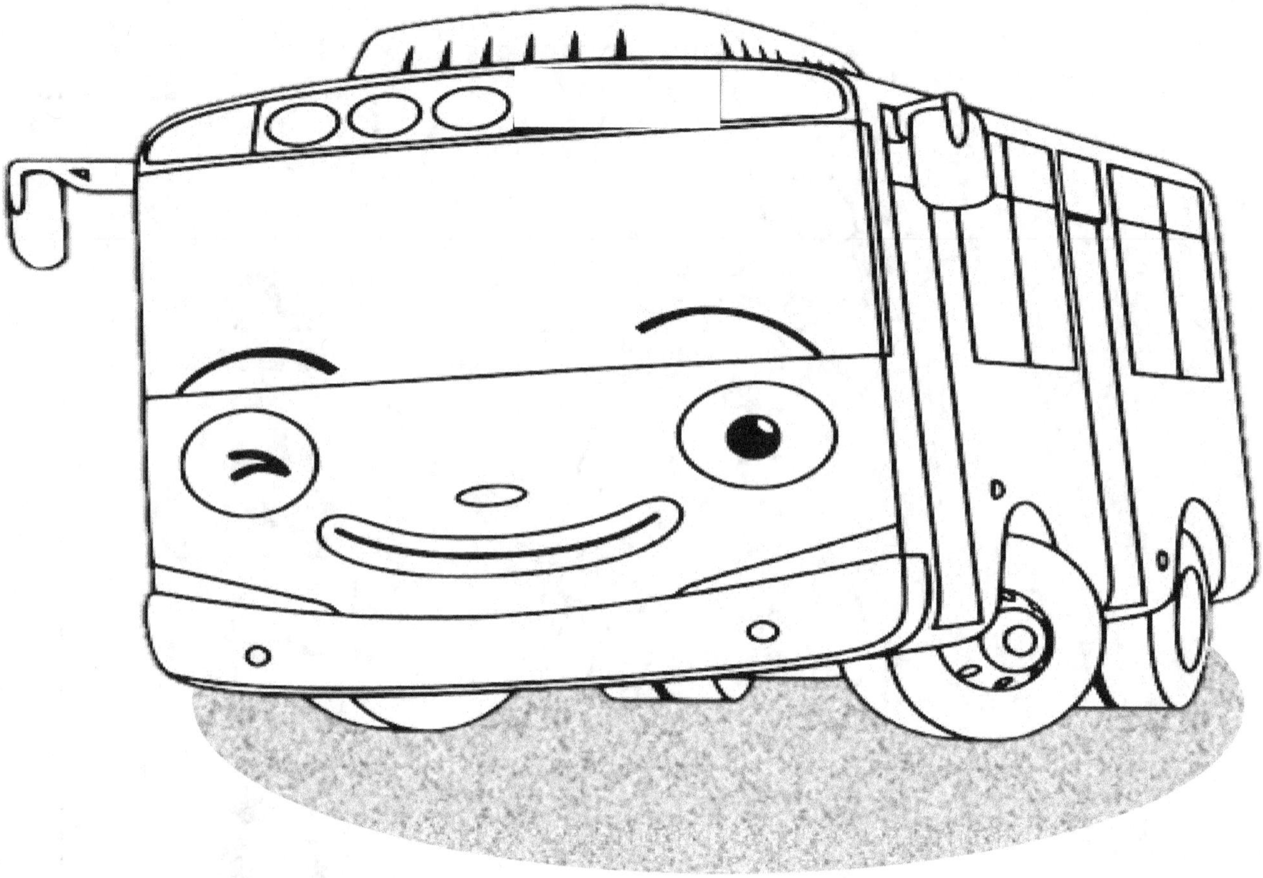

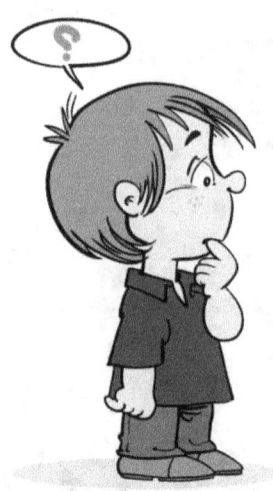 **[WE CALL THIS: ....]**

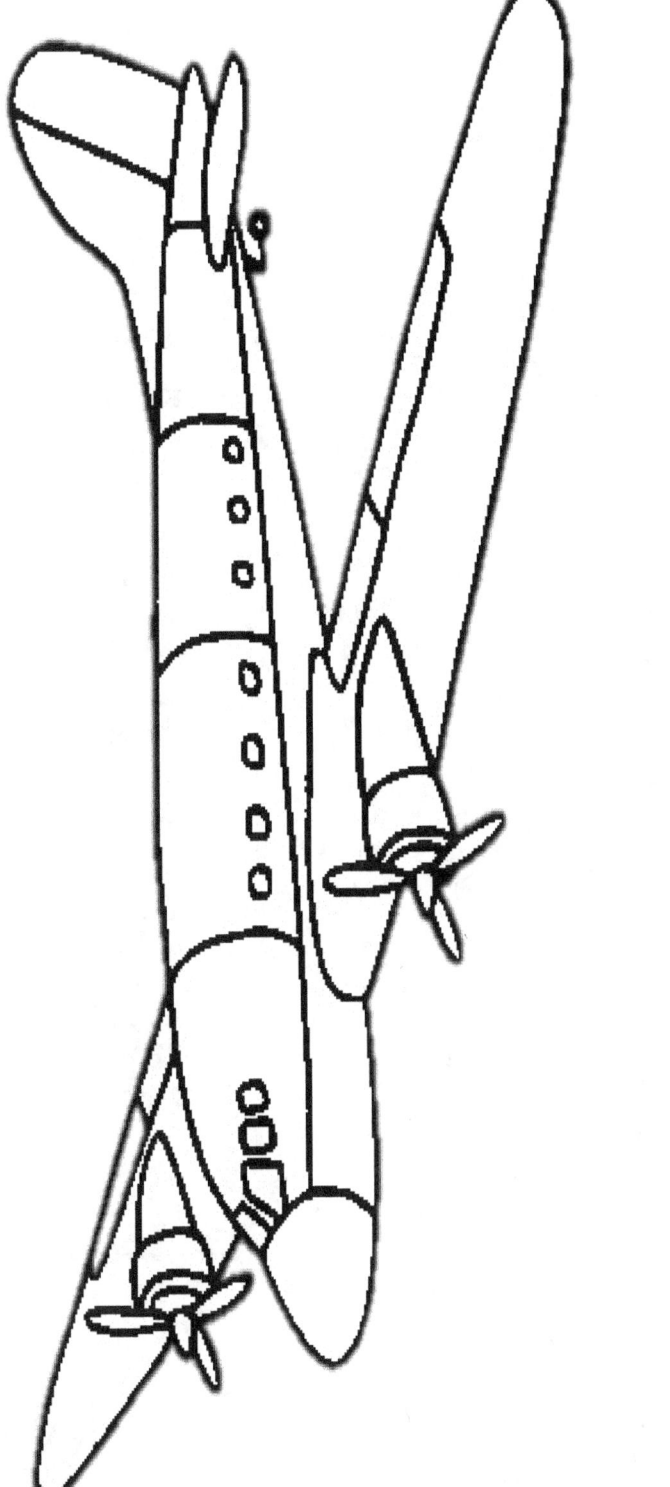

WE CALL THIS:

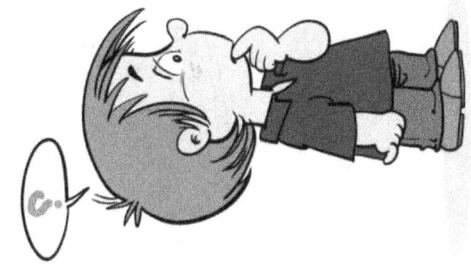

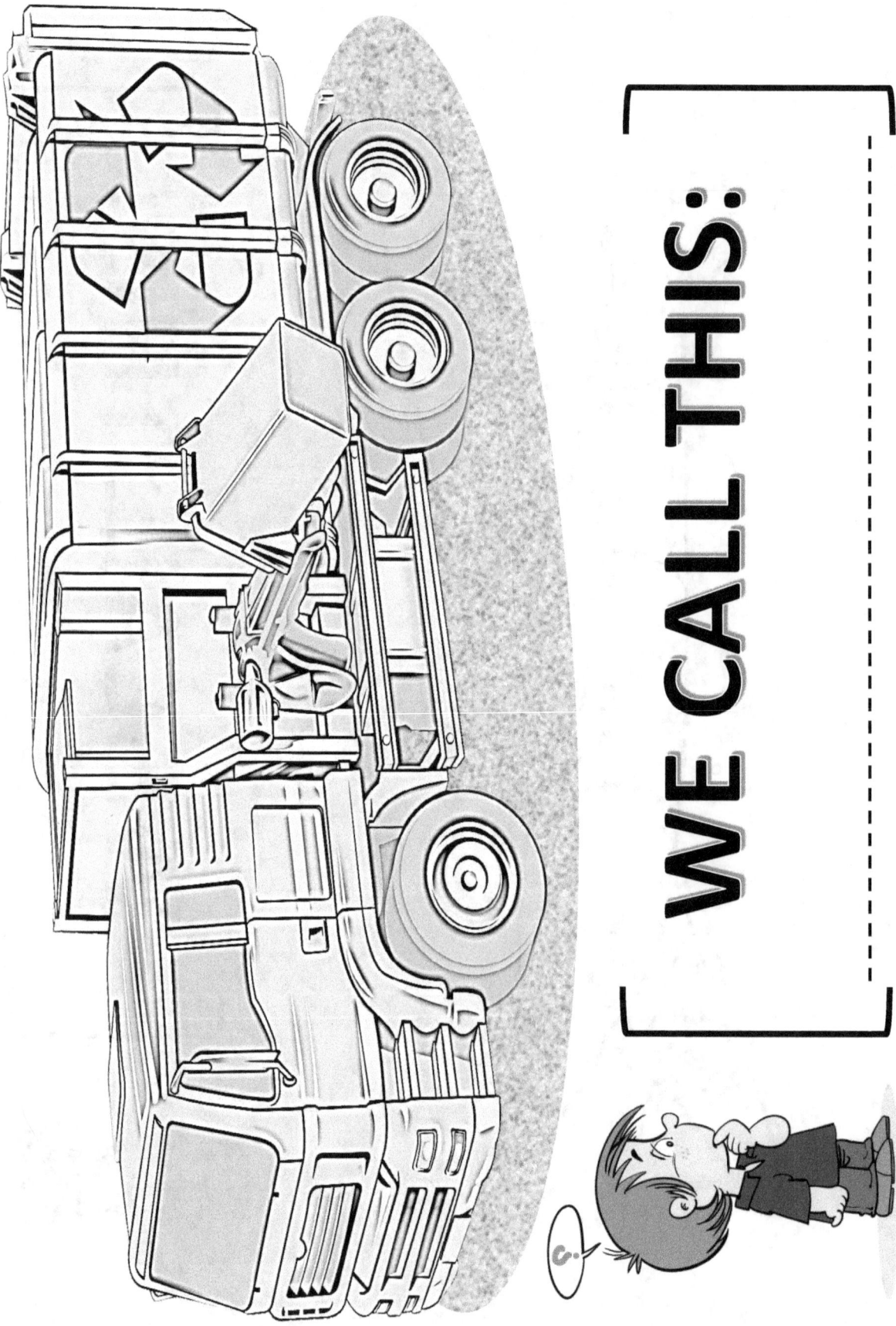

WE CALL THIS:

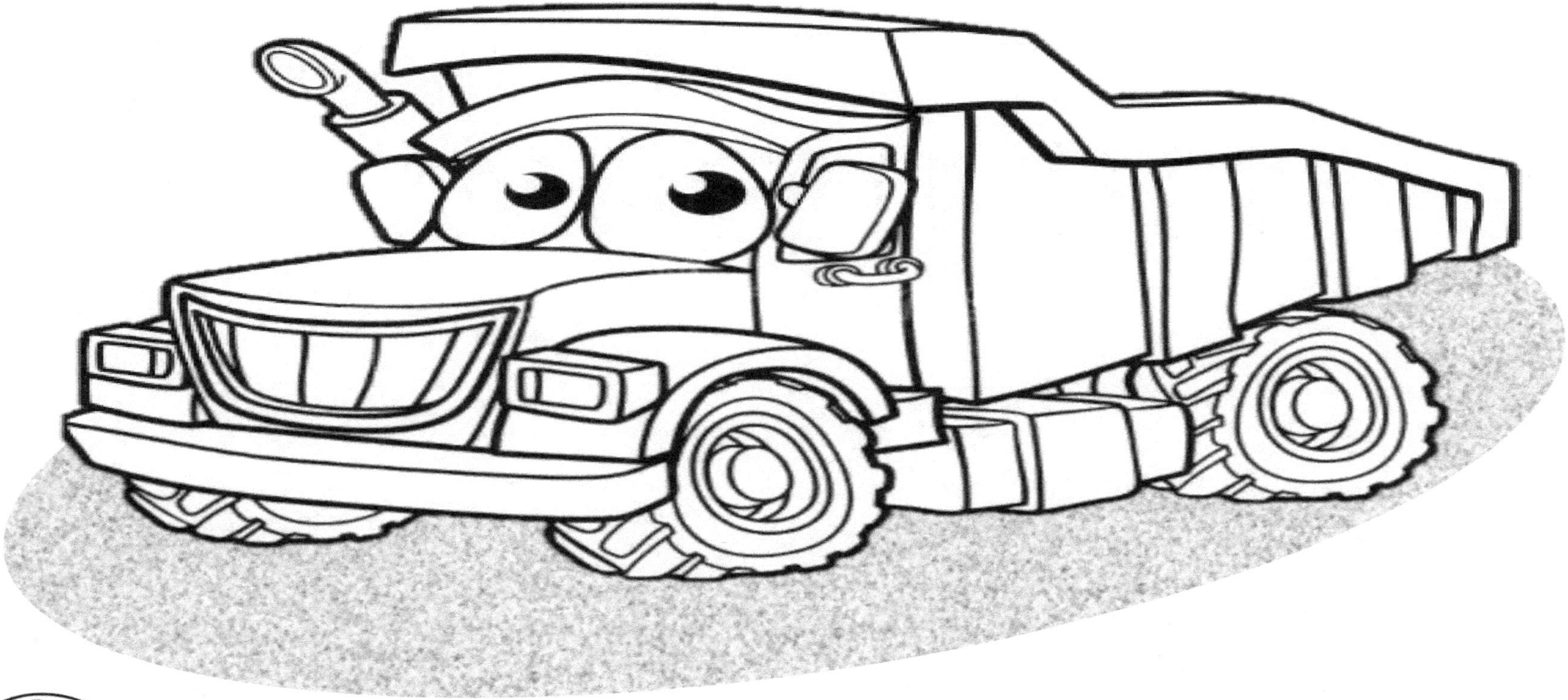

WE CALL THIS:

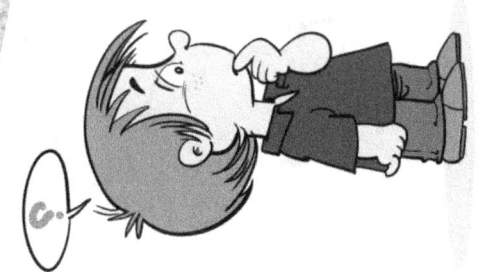

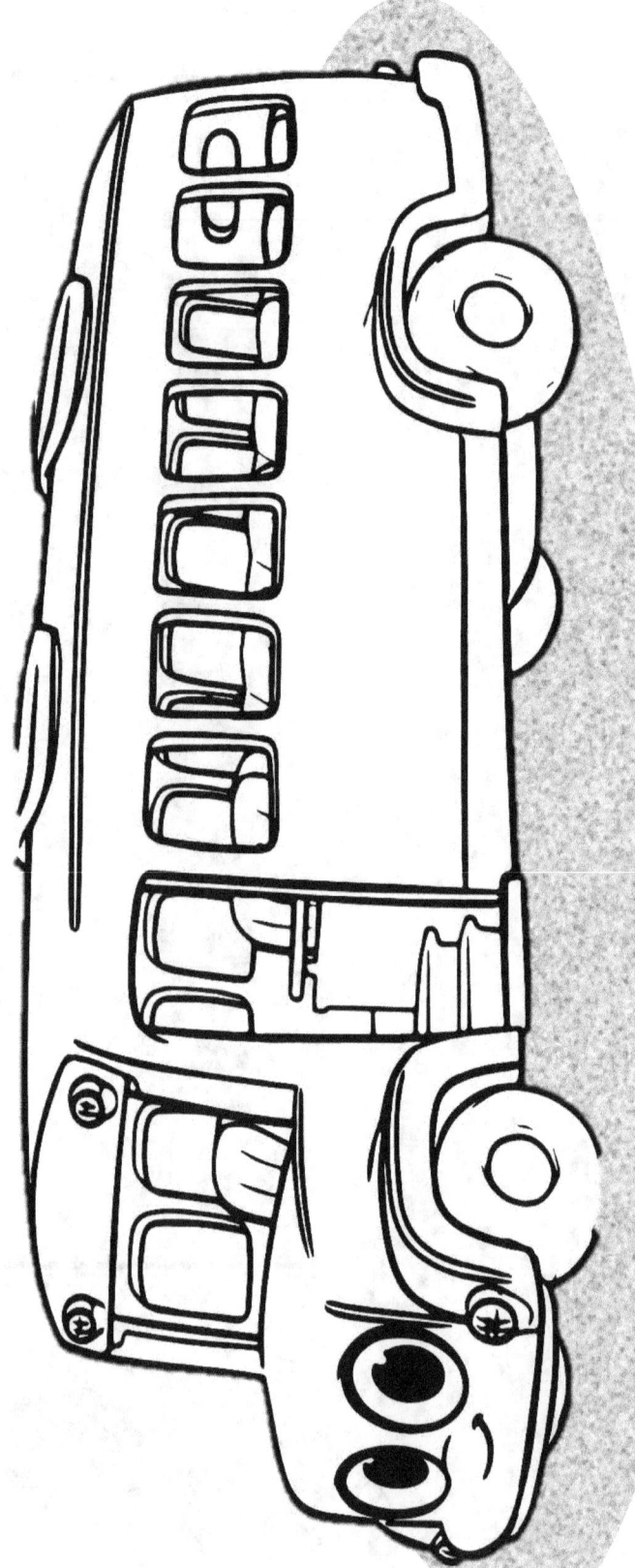

WE CALL THIS:

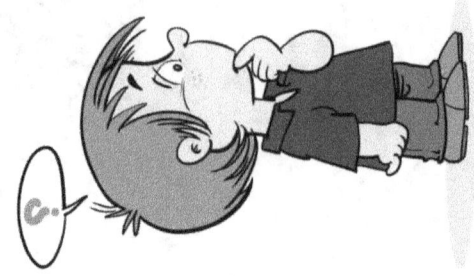

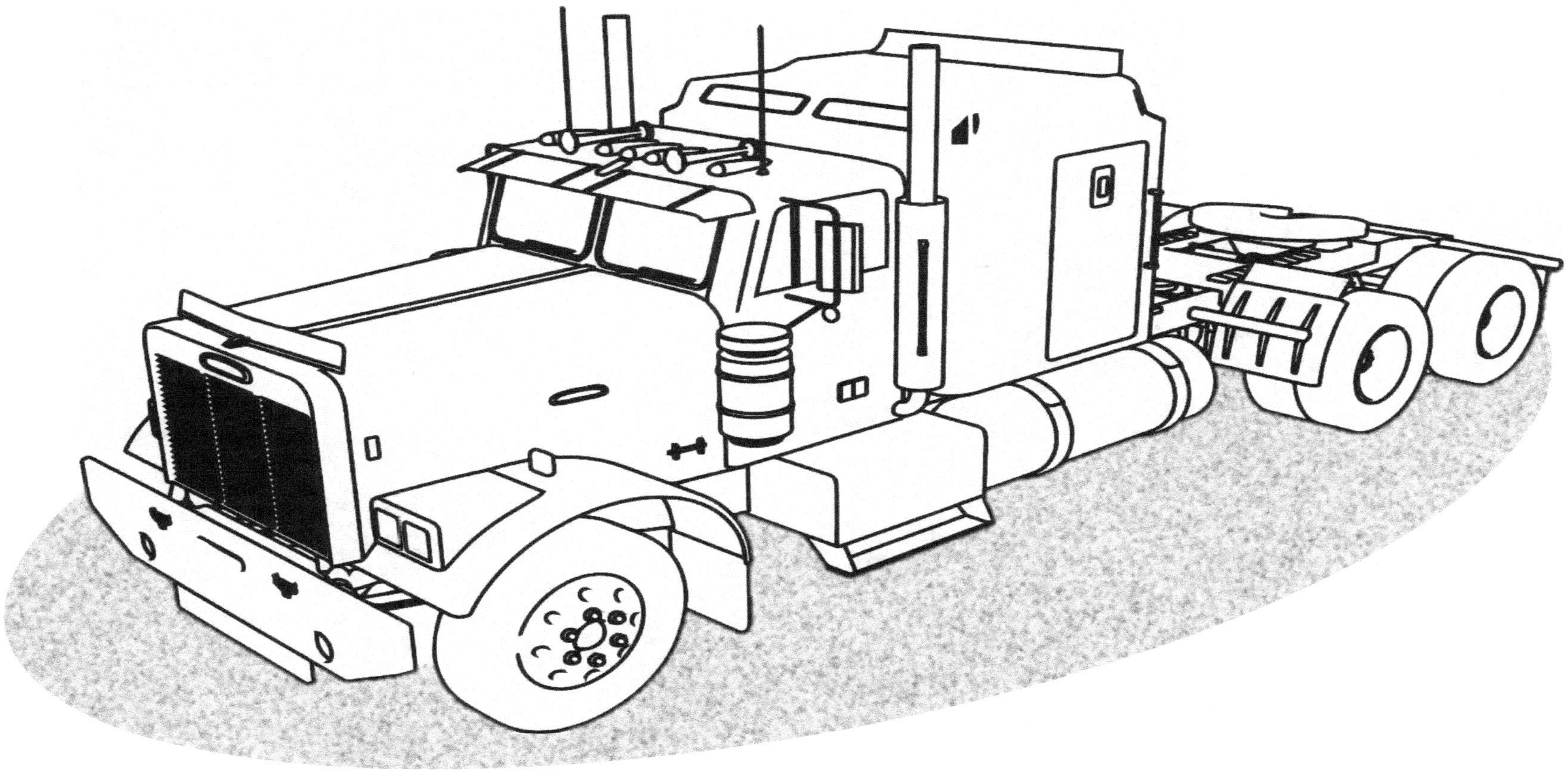

WE CALL THIS:

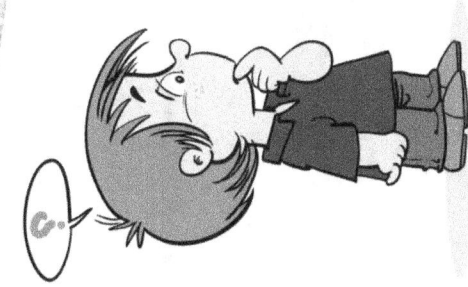

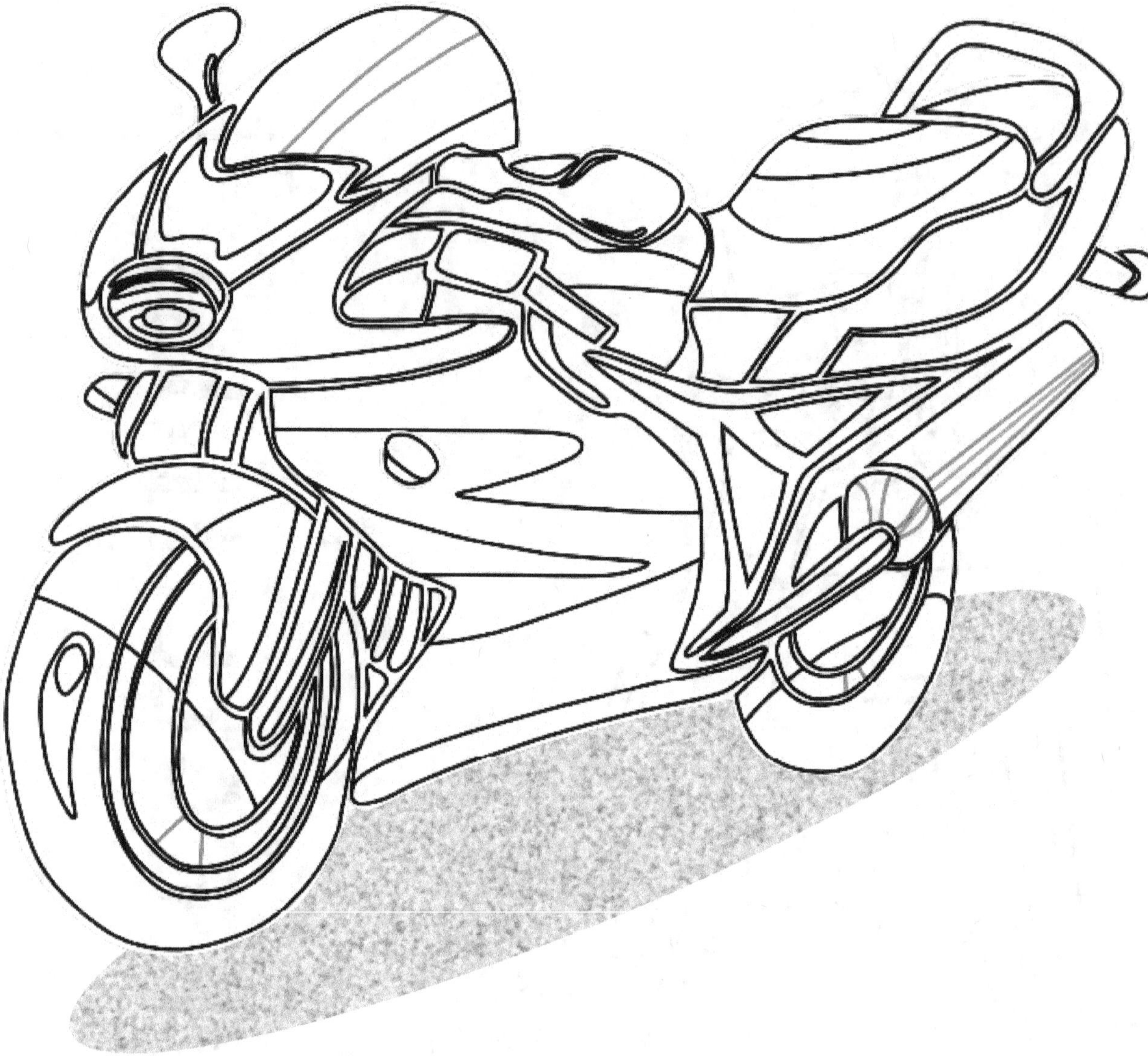

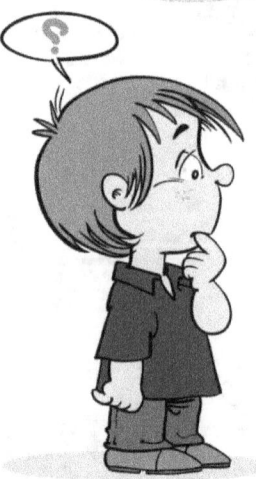

WE CALL THIS:

....

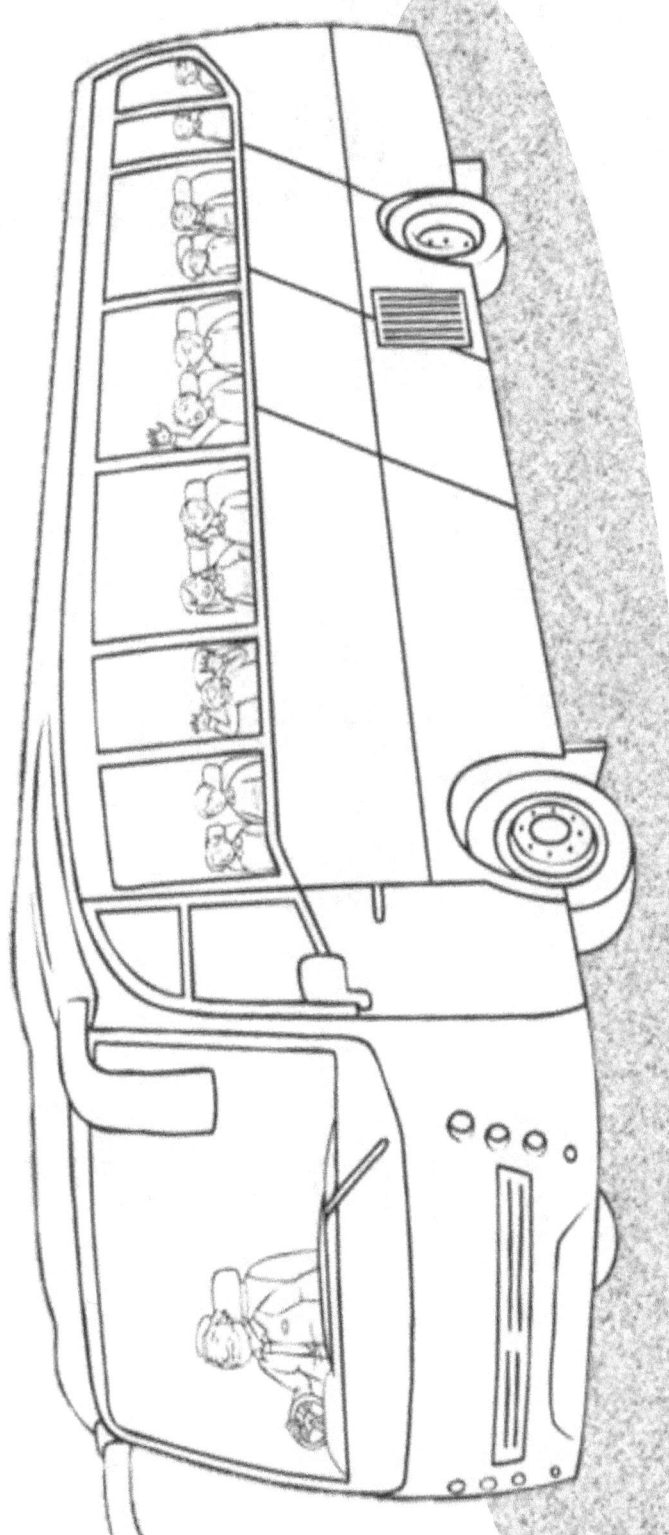

WE CALL THIS:

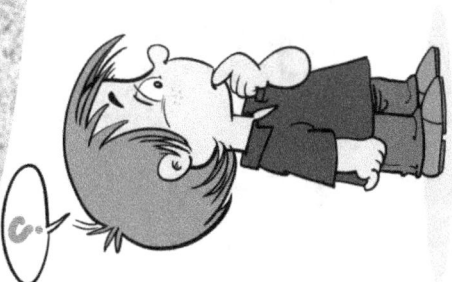

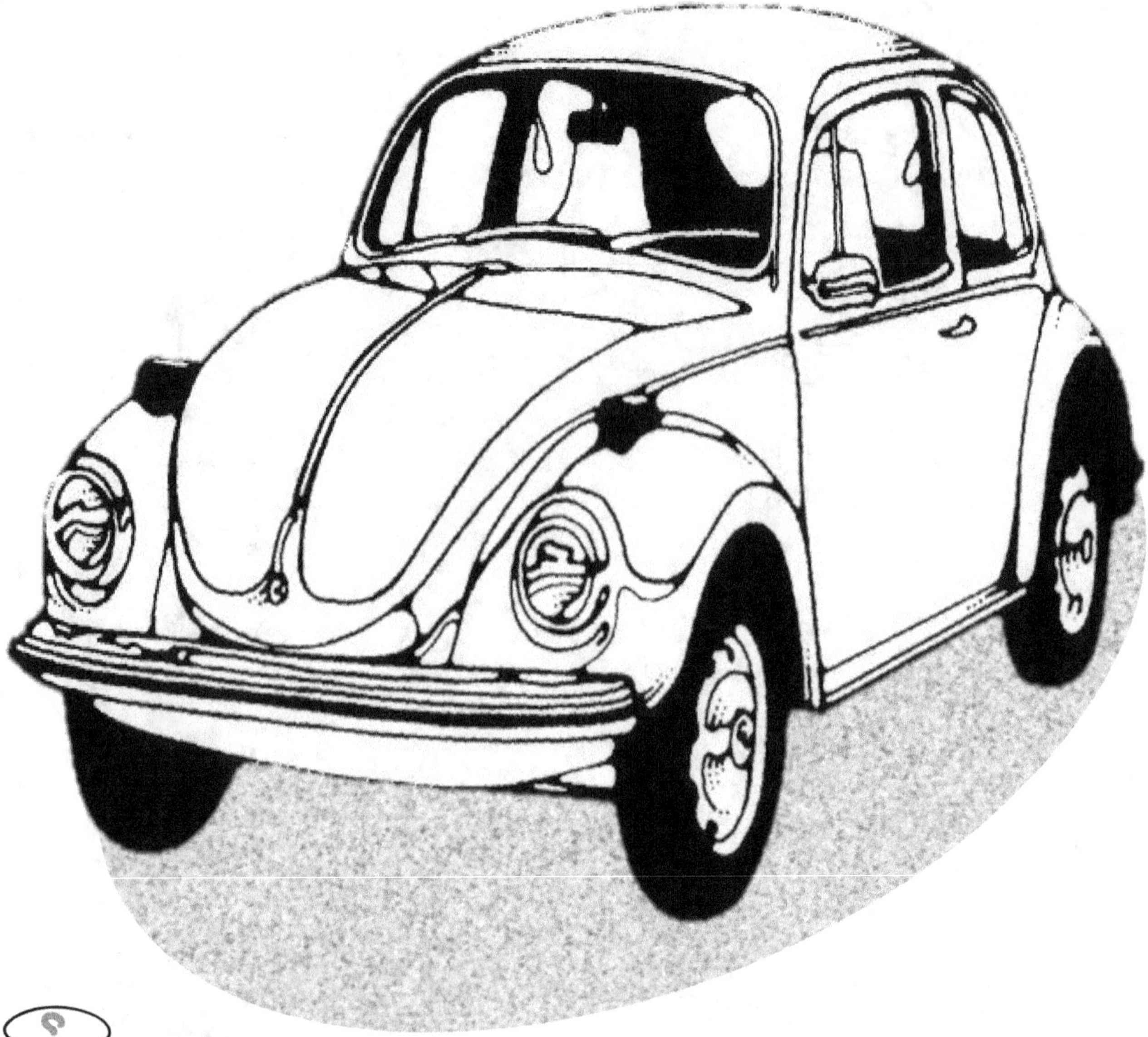

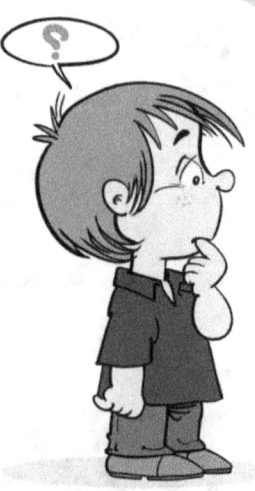 **WE CALL THIS:** ....

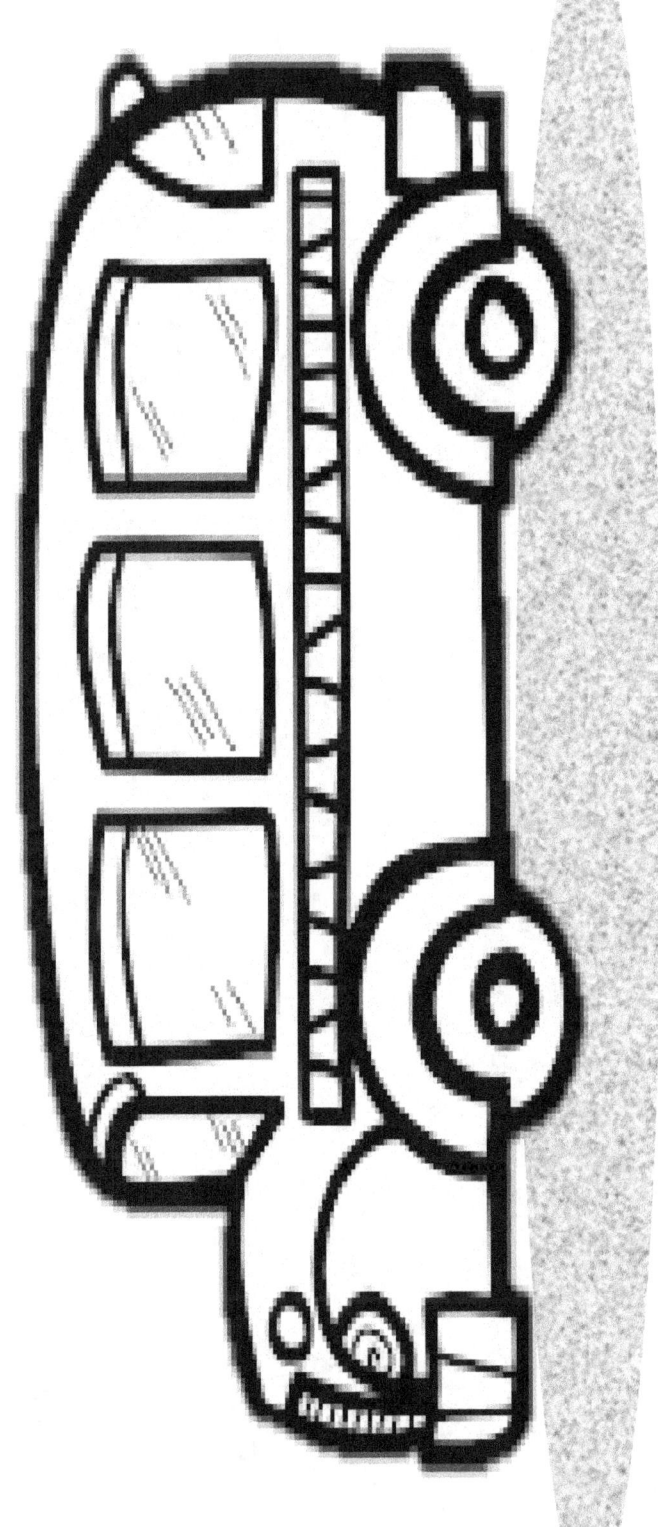

WE CALL THIS:

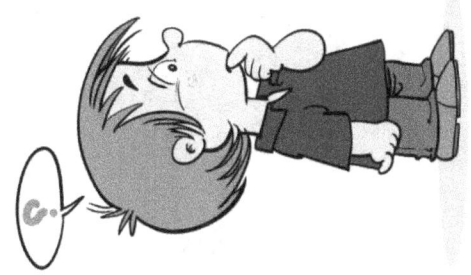

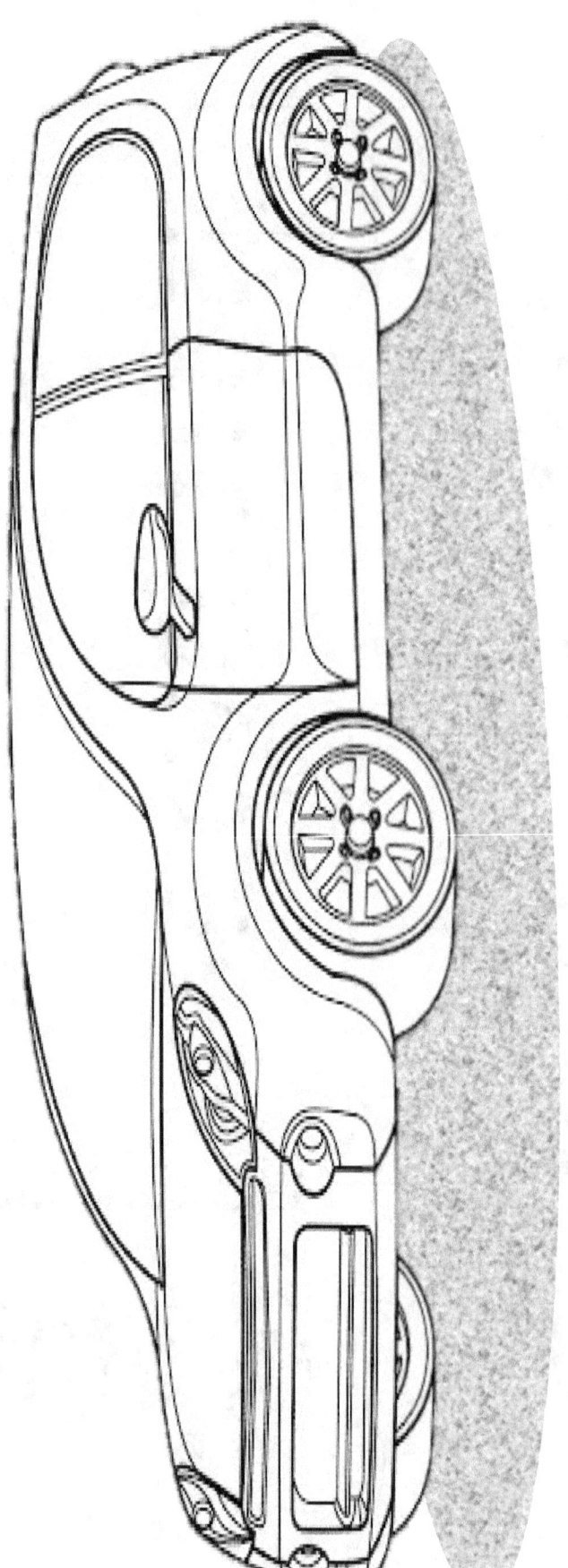

WE CALL THIS:

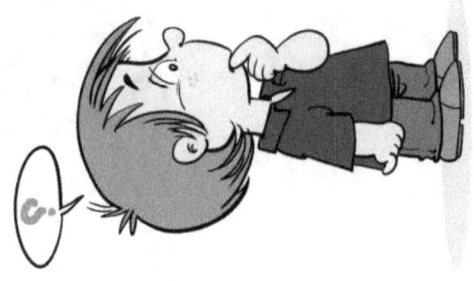

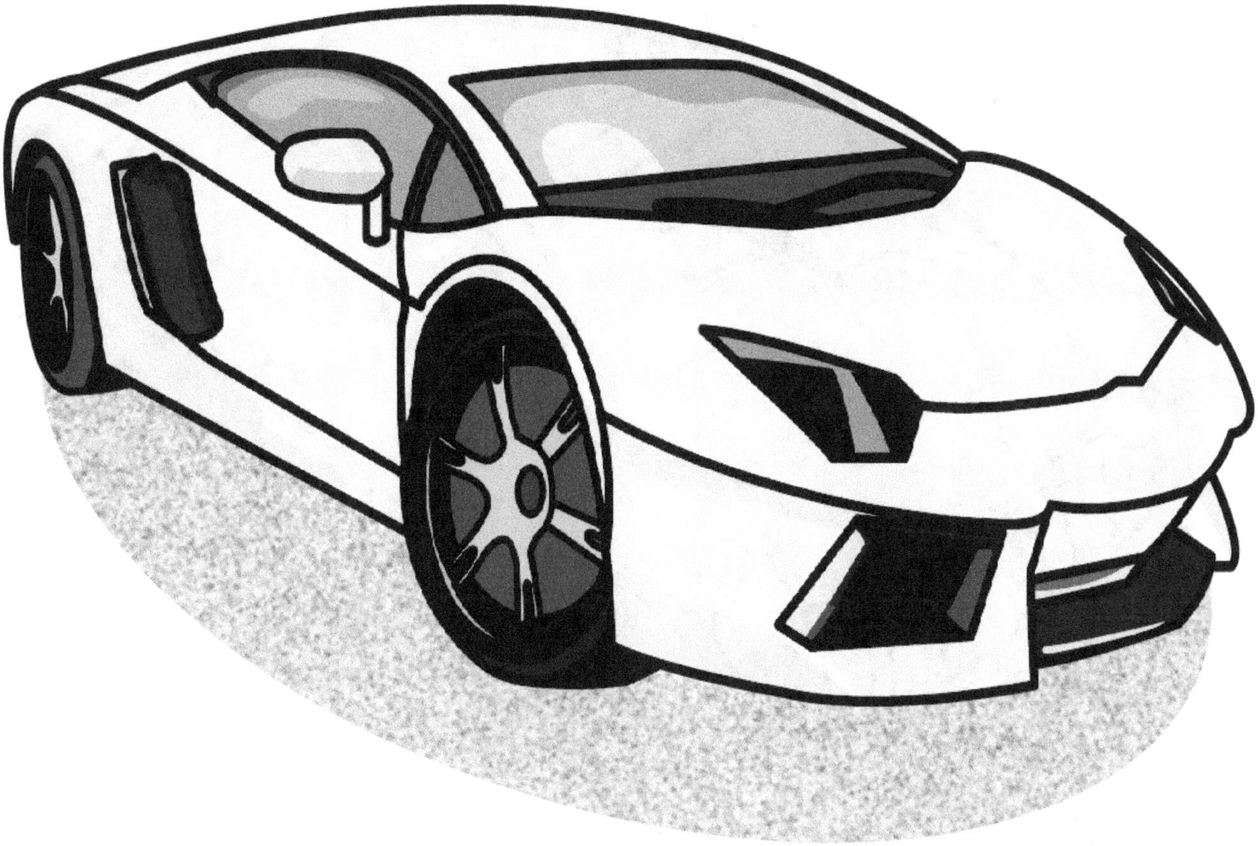

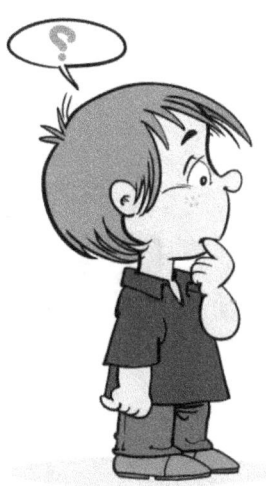

WE CALL THIS:

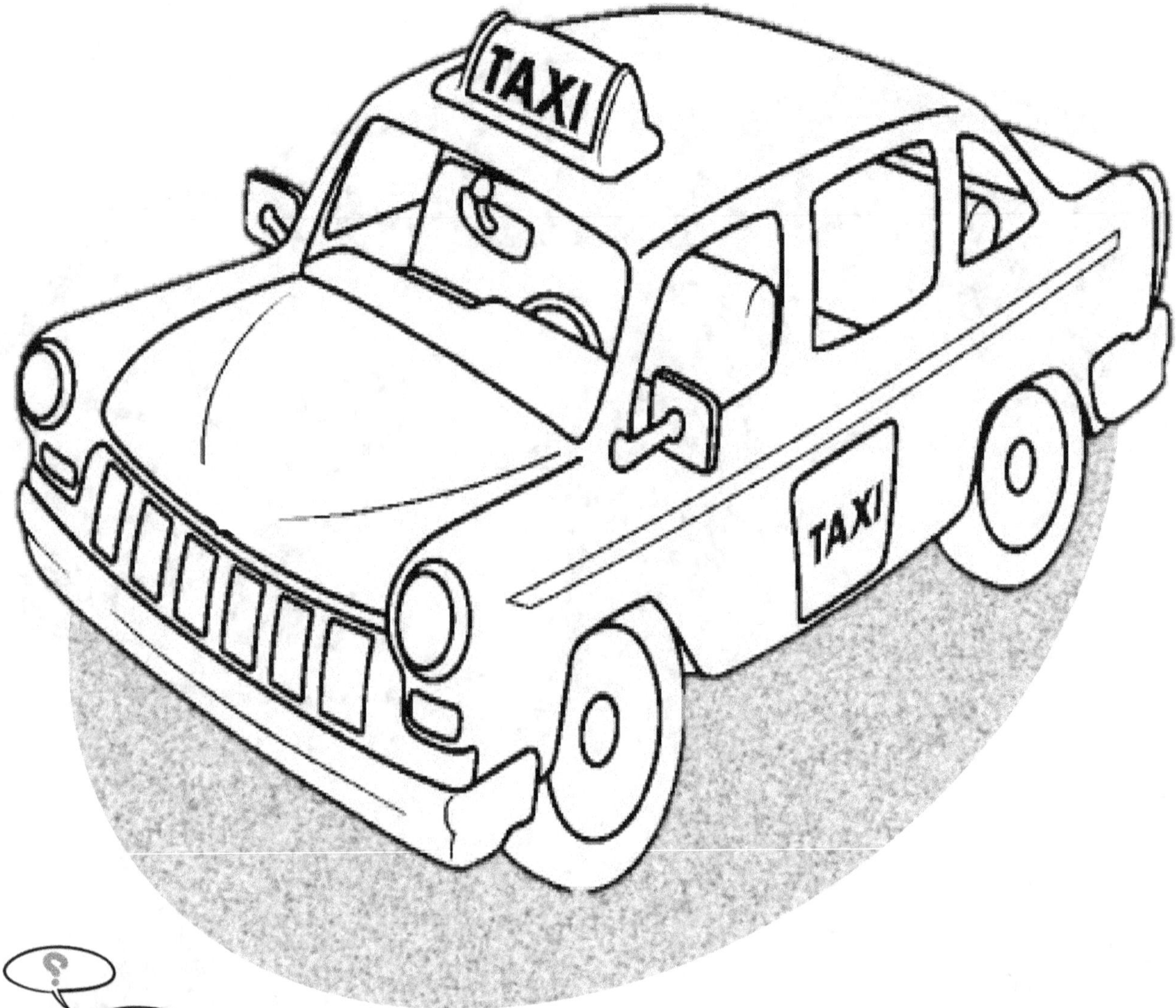

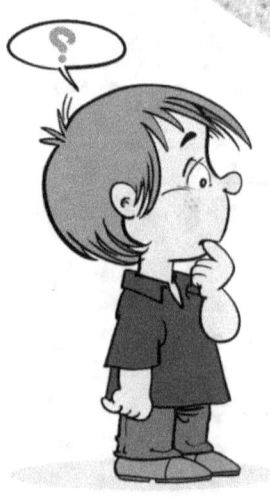

WE CALL THIS: _____

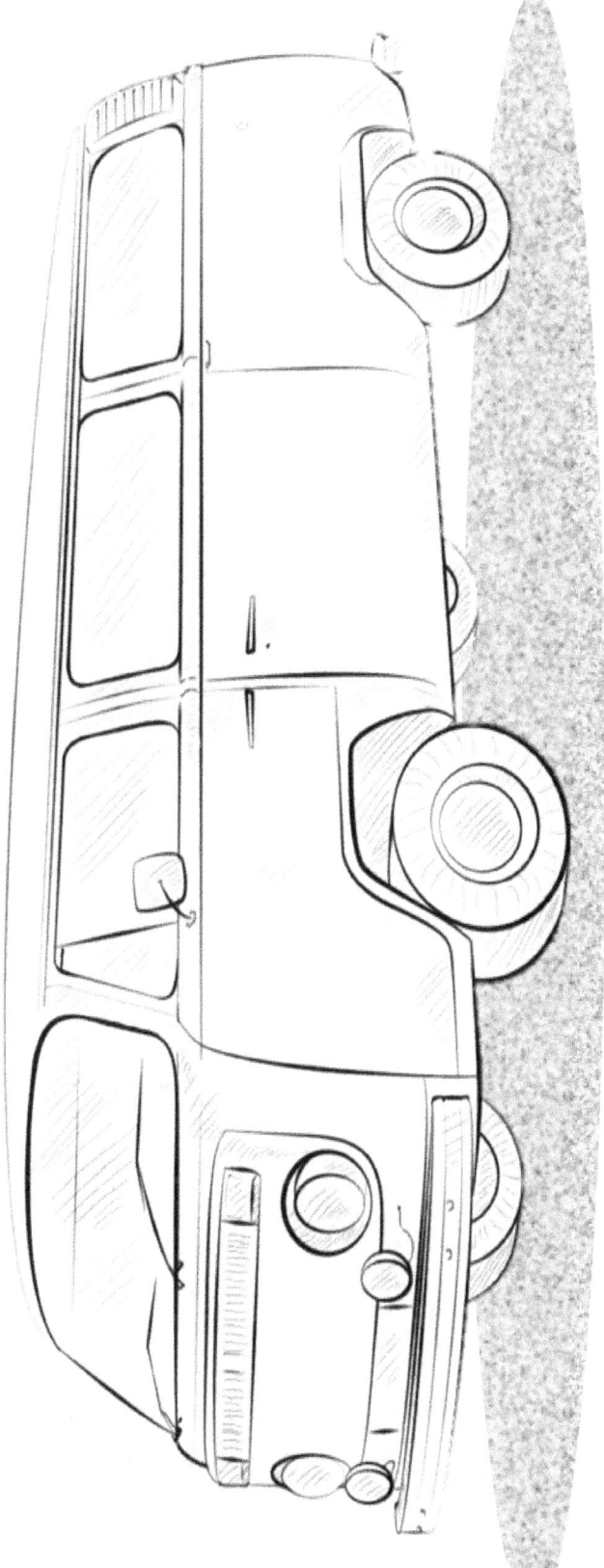

WE CALL THIS:

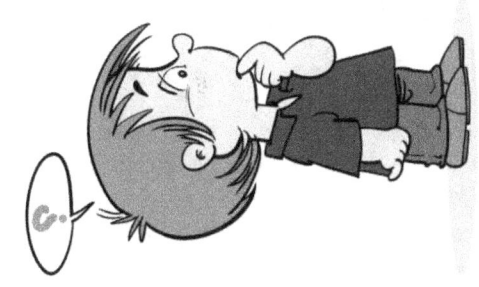

WE CALL THIS:

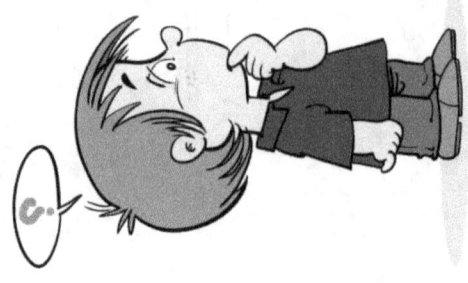

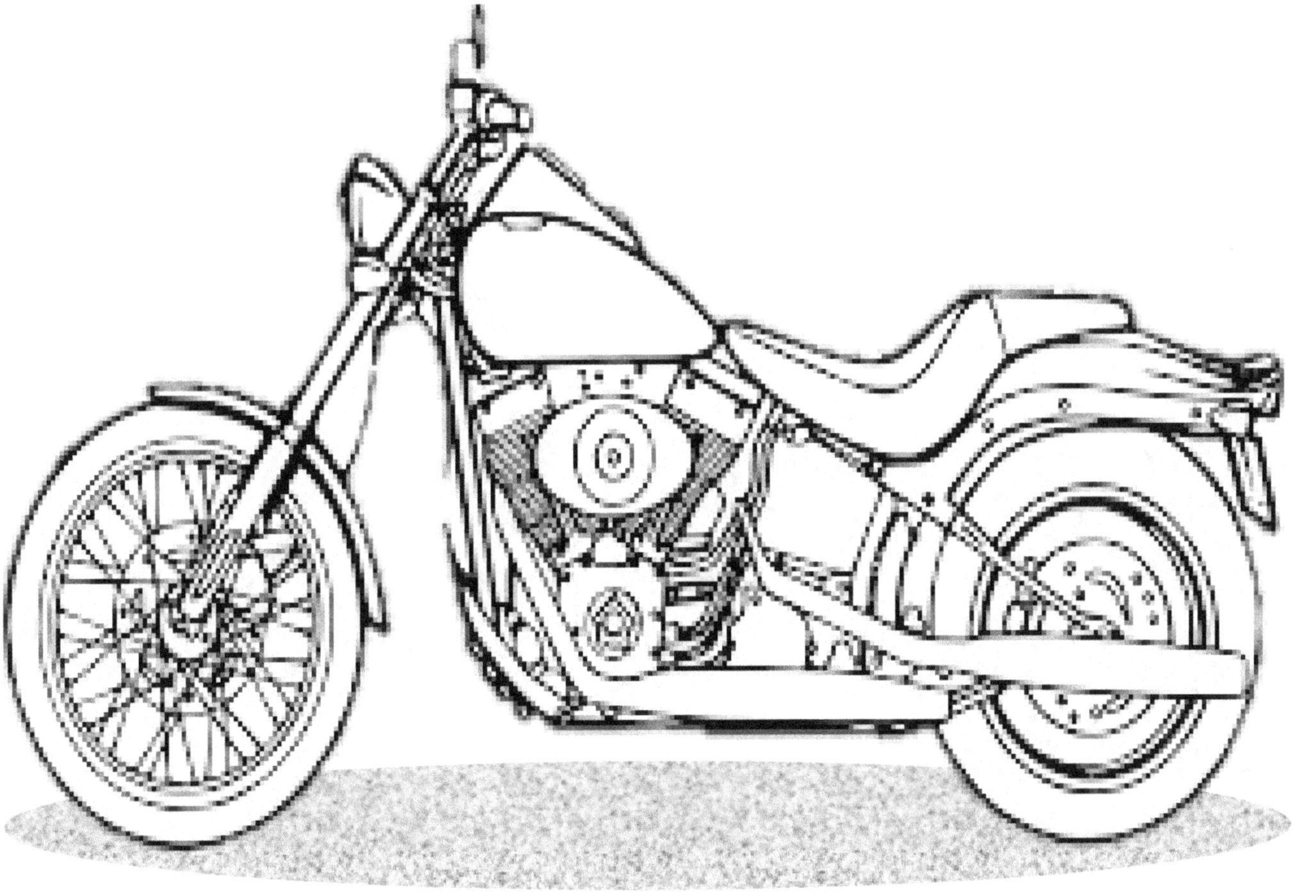

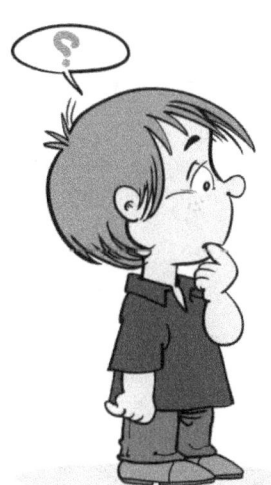

WE CALL THIS: